T0068225

the *Spirituality* of OTIS CLAYTON, SR.

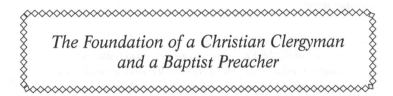

The Foundation of a Christian Clergyman
and a Baptist Preacher

Otis Clayton, Sr.

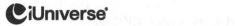

THE SPIRITUALITY OF OTIS CLAYTON, SR. THE FOUNDATION OF A CHRISTIAN CLERGYMAN AND A BAPTIST PREACHER

iUniverse books may be ordered through booksellers or by contacting:

iUniverse
1663 Liberty Drive
Bloomington, IN 47403
www.iuniverse.com
844-349-9409

ISBN: 978-1-6632-5664-5 (sc)
ISBN: 978-1-6632-5665-2 (e)

Library of Congress Control Number: 2023918603

Print information available on the last page.

iUniverse rev. date: 03/22/2024

CONTENTS

ESSAYS

POEMS

SERMONS

FOREWORD

I was born in rural Cross Plain, Tennessee, and I grew up in the home of a devoted Baptist Deacon and a Church Mother. I confess my Christian belief at an early age in the Friendship Missionary Baptist Church. I graduated from East Robertson High School and the American Baptist College in Nashville, Tennessee. While earning my degree there, I served as a bi-vocational pastor. I worked a job, supported my family, and served my congregation. For forty (40) years, I have served as the Senior Pastor at Saint John Missionary Baptist Church in Hendersonville, Tennessee.

My family members have supported this ministry untiredly for forty years of pastoral ministry. They include Rhonda McKisick-Bell, a devoted wife of forty-eight years; Demetria, my daughter; Demaria and Darrius; Gianna, my granddaughter; and other family members. Moreover, with God's help and the assistance of various ministers, I have accomplished some great things for God. We have developed and constructed the Robert Bell Fellowship Center to serve this metro community better. Furthermore, I have served the Middle Tennessee Baptist Missionary Education as the

Vice-President and the Moderator for the East Fork District Association.

But, let me say something significant about my brother and friend, Dr. Otis Clayton Sr. I firmly believe that this book, "The Spirituality of Otis Clayton Sr: The Foundation of a Christian Clergyman and a Baptist Preacher," needs to be read by every Christian and every person of faith. He discusses his Christian convictions and his reading and studying our faith traditions. In this capacity, he served over twenty (20) years wearing and serving as a Chaplain in the United States Army. He matriculated from a patriotic American family. His parents had nine children: four (4) daughters and five (5) sons. Dr. Clayton and his other brothers reflected this patriotism because they all served honorably wearing the United States Armed Forces.

Indeed, he is a strong advocate that every Christian, especially clergymen, must study to show themselves approved as servants of God. The clergyperson must prepare for effective Christian leadership and service. Furthermore, he has served as a pastor of several Eastern Arkansas and Northern Mississippi congregations. Like all of us, Dr. Clayton has had his highs, lows, trials, and tribulations. He is a divorcee, but divorce is something that he is not proud of because he did not get married to go to divorce court. Dr. Clayton is a devoted father of two children and several grandchildren. He is an avid writer and researcher because he has published several books. Nonetheless, Dr. Clayton highlights that, though he is a creative artist, he has not given up on trying to find a love relationship with a woman of faith, even in a foreign country in South America like Colombia.

Most importantly, Dr. Clayton demonstrates his sensitivity to women in ministry and his diversity as a scholar who is essentially a preacher. In this book, he dedicates a sermon to the founders of the Porch, a community organization for writers in metro Nashville. As an example of his versatility as a writer, he writes poetry. But he uses poetry to demonstrate his ability as a preacher to move God's people.

Dr. Clayton and I have been dear friends for the last several years. But I feel that we have been friends all of our lives. This is because Dr. Clayton never meets a stranger. We became fast friends when I met him when he moved to Hendersonville, Tennessee, from Aurora, Colorado. He moved her closer to family, especially his devoted Mother, Elizabeth Murphy-Clayton. She lived in his hometown of Memphis, Tennessee.

But she had become weaker because of her illnesses. The COVID-19 pandemic did not deter him from demonstrating his love for Mother Elizabeth. Dr. Clayton gave her a surprise birthday party in the driveway of his home. He asks me to use a few tables and chairs from our Saint John Missionary Baptist Church. Mother Elizabeth adopted me as one of her many sons at that time. Now, this is one of the reasons Why Dr. Clayton calls me his brother by another Mother.

In his book, Dr. Clayton reveals what he is made of. He is a Christian clergyman but primarily a good preacher in the African American preaching tradition. His earned doctorate in homiletics from Vanderbilt

University reflects the best in that tradition. Dr. Clayton's book must be read by both those in the pulpit and the pews.

Reverend Robert Bell
Senior Pastor, Saint John Missionary Baptist Church
Hendersonville, Tennessee

INTRODUCTION

I was called at the early age of ten to become involved in the ministry. My oldest aunt, Willie Mae McGowan (Sister), was pivotal in my decision. She was an evangelist in the Holiness Pentecostal Church. Sister always took with her children and other children in the neighborhood whenever she went to church. So, I went with Sister and her children, my first cousin, to a Holiness Pentecostal Revival. But, if truth be told, women have always played leading roles within the church but have traditionally not been acknowledged. The same can also be said that women generally have only sometimes been accepted in the larger community.

Nonetheless, Sister or Aunt Willie Mae always led the devotional service. She sang, read scripture, prayed, and played even the tambourine in her church services.

Further, my parents married at an early age. My father was eighteen years old, and my mother was just fifteen years of age. Therefore, they could not complete high school because of their marriage and family obligations. However, they had nine children: four daughters and five sons. They ensured their children never forgot the meaning, value, and significance of obtaining the best education possible. They preached and taught us that getting a quality education was invaluable. They repeated endlessly, "The mind is a terrible thing to waste." So, my Father had the ambition that I would become a lawyer for several reasons. They include that I would use the law to help protect the rights of people, especially African Americans, and I would use the legal system to help protect other persons in the criminal justice system. My Father became a bootlegger of corn whiskey, which in and of itself was illegal. Unfortunately, my parents began to have endless arguments and misunderstandings. It always centered around my father's inability to stop gambling, selling corn whiskey, and his growing abusive behavior towards my beloved mother.

My mother eventually became tired of being tired. She separated and left my father and took her nine children with her. However, when my parents separated and divorced, I had to grow up immediately and forgo my love for playing basketball at Booker T. Washington High School for my high school. It is the oldest high school for African Americans in West Tennessee. Nevertheless, at 16, I was in the 10th grade. My mother was injured on her job and had surgery on both hands. My oldest sister had become pregnant. Therefore, I needed to secure full-time employment to survive as a family. I secured a subsequent job at Southern Central Paper Company. I worked throughout high school from 3 p.m. until 11 p.m. nightly.

So, this book is about how I have grown spiritually

to understand my calling and purpose in life. Still, in the process, I have become more sensitive to women's needs, concerns, challenges, and tribulations. My beloved Mother's experiences and my association with the Porch have helped me immeasurably with feminist issues and the marginalized persons who make up our world.

Essays

MY CALL TO THE MINISTRY

I was called into the ministry at the age of ten. It was several weeks after I had decided to become a follower of Christ. Shortly thereafter, I informed my fraternal grandfather, Silas Clayton Sr, about my conversion experience. I stated "I attended the revival meeting at the New Nonconnah Missionary Baptist Church. The Reverend Robert Lee Jones, the Senior Pastor, invited another local pastor to serve as the evangelist for his church's summer revival. I was one of ten to twenty young adolescents and teenagers who were candidates on the mourner's bench. After the evangelist's sermon, he asked each candidate to stand up to confess the faith. Then, he asked, "Yes or No? Do you accept Christ as our personal savior?" I said, "Yes! I accept Christ as my personal savior. I decided to become more like Christ in every aspect of my life. Last Sunday, I was baptized and accepted as a New Nonconnah Missionary Baptist Church member."

After our conversation, my grandfather, whom we also called affectionately Papa, advised that my conversion experience was of no effect or meaningful. He stated, "Son, I must tell you this one thing. When you accept Christ into your life, you must feel something. So, I want you to return to the mourner's bench and not get off it until you feel something."

I grew up and spent my youth and adolescence in the rural southwest community of Shelby County, Tennessee. This community was grounded religiously in a fusion of evangelical and holiness Pentecostal Christianity. It was not unusual to hear believers speak in different tongues. I had problems with glossolalia. It made no sense to me. In this respect, those believers who practiced glossolalia placed tremendous emphasis not only on the Gospels test, which speaks about the person and works of Christ. But, in contrast, they place razor-like focus on the Book of Acts, specifically on Chapter 2. The primary center of attention of this text is on the movement of the spirit. It reveals the movement and growth of the Christian faith and churches.

Weekly, I was in and out of various churches. If my mother did not take me and my siblings to church, we were taken mostly by other female members of my extended family. One summer evening, I attended this holiness Pentecostal revival meeting. I went there with my several of my fraternal aunties and a host of first cousins. Pastor Elder Lusk was the host minister who was a byproduct of his culture. As such, he regularly exercised patriarchal and misogynistic tendencies. While at this revival meeting, Elder Lusk asked all the boys present to stand up and come to the altar for prayer. He said, "God told me that one of your boys here has been called to preach. I do not know who you are. But God knows who you are." Elder Lusk prayed out loud as we stood there in a powerful and moving voice. He laid hands and anointed me and my cousins' heads with oil.

In all honesty, I felt the call, at that time, to become a minister. But I said nothing. This was not because I was terrified nor was I afraid to publicly announce my call to Pastor Lusk nor to his congregation. I wanted him or someone to explain the call to ministry in a rational and sensible manner. Since I never obtained an explanation of the call from a religious leader and or fellow believer, I avoided any mention of my call.

It was not until I volunteered to become an airman in the United States Air Force that I learned what the call to ministry entailed. At that time, I was stationed at the Seymour Johnson Air Force Base in Goldsboro, North Carolina. I met my first Chaplain who also happened to be an African American Baptist clergyman. He was multi-talented because he could pray, preach, and was a gifted musician. However, we served as members of the Base Honor Guard Detail, which allowed us to spend some invaluable time getting to know one another personally. When the opportunity presented itself, I inquired that he explained, "What was the call to ministry regards?" The Chaplain replied, "The call to ministry is to serve God and God's people by preparing oneself to serve as a spiritual leader."

Shortly thereafter, I publicly announced my call to the ministry, came off active duty, and became a graduate student in religion at the Memphis Theological Seminary. After graduation, I was ordained by my home church as a Baptist clergyman, received an ecclesiastical endorsement from the National Baptist Church Convention, USA Incorporated, and obtained a direct commission as a Chaplain in the United States Army.

MY UNIQUE PERSONALITY: A PREACHER LOOKING FOR A GENUINE LOVE RELATIONSHIP

Hello! I hope and pray that all is well with you, your charming family members, and your dear friends.

I want to thank my dear friend, the brother, whose name I will not mention, and his entire staff for this delightful opportunity. They requested that I make this statement about My Unique Personality. However, for the purpose of this book, I call my unique personality: The Preacher Looking for a Genuine Love Relationship. My personality and calling as a preacher of the gospel make Me the person I am. If my memory serves correctly, no other person is like me. Hahaha!

I will discuss several things about my personality, which will signal to someone in my viewing and listening audience that we have mutual interests. If that is true, I look forward to seeing, meeting, and discussing our mutual interests with you in the immediate future. I have several things to share with You about my unique personality. They include (1) some of my unique values, (2) some of my unique interests, (3) some of my unique hobbies, and (4) some of my unique qualities.

I have some unique values. They are (1) Faith, (2) Love, (3) Education, (4) Leadership, and (5) Hope. **Faith.** I am a member of the clergy, a Baptist minister, and a preacher. This means that I am a person of faith in the Protestant Christian tradition. Do you remember that "Faith is the substance of things hoped for and the evidence of things not seen" (Hebrews 11:1)? Are You also a Woman of Faith?

Love. Love is another pivotal value that I possess. The Greek language breaks down the concept of love in three areas. They are **Eros**, **Phila**, and **Agape**. I have decided to become a serious member of My Colombian Wife for essentially one primary reason. I am seeking to locate and identify that Special Woman for Me. I want to fall in love with her, enjoy an abiding, passionate, romantic relationship, and live in a committed and serious relationship with her. Is someone in this video audience willing and ready to fall in love with Me? Hahaha!

Phila is the kind of love that I have for my family. My family consists of my mother, children, grandchildren, other family members, dear friends, and members of my faith community.

Agape Love is the kind of love God has for us all. Since God loves us, I have entered a love relationship with God. I ask God to help me in everything that I try to do. God has demonstrated God's love for Me. God so loved the world that God gave us Jesus Christ, and whoever believes in

Christ will not perish but have everlasting life (John 3:16). "Falling in love with Jesus is the best thing I have ever done. In Jesus' arms, I feel connected. In Jesus' arms, I am never disconnected. In Jesus' arms, I feel connected. Falling in love with Jesus is the best thing that I have ever done." Hopefully, I will meet that special woman through my membership who shares this understanding of love with me.

Education. Education is another one of my significant values. I believe "The mind is a terrible thing to waste." In short, I value education because it was a crime to teach an African American to read or write. But that is no longer the case in America today. The Fourteenth Amendment of the United States Constitution abolished slavery. This amendment gave freedom to all African Americans to become whatever they wished.

I thank God that I and all people in America, regardless of race, creed, color, and religious persuasion, can now attend and pursue a quality education. I can hear renowned author James Baldwin say, "You were born into a society which spelled out with brutal clarity, and in as many ways as possible, that you were a worthless human being." But I refused to accept what society has said about me and my people. I have worked tirelessly to earn advanced degrees, which includes a doctoral degree from Vanderbilt University. Oh Yes! I am a living witness to what quality education can achieve for any individual.

Leadership. Leadership is a value that I embrace. General Colin Powell maintained that "Leadership is solving problems." I did that for my country, the United States of America. For twenty (20) years, I served as a United States Army Officer, and in this capacity, I was the Chaplain for thousands of members of the United States Armed Forces. I served as their Spiritual leader. Of course, when I develop a potential relationship with my significant other, I look forward to explaining more of my understanding of leadership and learning about her understanding of leadership.

Hope. Hope is an important value. President Barack Obama, the poet Maya Angelou, and Vice-President Kamala Harris are helpful as I explain my own perspective on this concept called "hope." Obama says, "Hope is the belief that destiny will not be written for us, but by us, by the men and women who are not content to settle for the world as it is, who dare to remake the world as it should be." Angelou remarks, "Hope and fear cannot occupy the same space. Invite one to stay." Harris states, "The need (exists today) to restore hope for residents who are struggling in Central American nations."

Like Kamala Harris, Maya Angelou, and Barack Obama, I have my own understating of hope. For me, hope is never giving up or giving in to whatever trials and tribulations that I face. I believe behind every Night in the morning, the sun will rise and shine. I believe behind every Thunderstorm, there is a beautiful Rainbow. Glory Hallelujah! Glory Hallelujah! So, I will, and I must always keep hope alive.

Next, besides unique values, I also have some unique interests. They are (1) good stories to tell, (2) Charisma, (3) living an interesting life, and (4) concerned about the welfare of others. **Good stories**. I have good stories to tell. These are stories that have been passed on to me by my elders. This is one of the reasons why I enjoy reading about my family history, African American History, and World History. This reading about history provides and allows me to learn other stories to tell.

Charisma. Charisma is something that interests me. I am a preacher who enjoys inspiring, encouraging, and motivating others always to do their best in all their endeavors. Jesus says, "The Spirit of the Lord is on me because God has anointed me to proclaim good news to the poor. God has sent me to proclaim freedom for the prisoners and recovery of sight for the blind, to set the oppressed free" (Luke 4:18). This kind of charisma deeply interests me.

Living an interesting life. I live an interesting and arresting life. My life is an open book since it includes visiting the world to see different cultures and meeting new people. Over the last three months, I have visited three different continents: (1) Africa, (2) Europe, and (3) South America. And, before this year concludes, I look forward to visiting other continents. Is not traveling and visiting other continents interesting to You?

Concerned about the welfare of others. As indicated earlier, I am a clergy member who adheres, like Jesus Christ, to the philosophy of altruism. This is working tirelessly and endlessly to help others. Like Jesus, I am deeply concerned about the welfare of others, specifically those who are dispossessed, marginalized, and experiencing emotional or spiritual troubles. I learned recently that a former married parishioner of mine suddenly lost his wife. She had been his devoted wife for nearly fifty years, the devoted mother of their three children, and the grandmother of their grandchildren. This family lived nearly three (300) hundred miles from my residence. Nonetheless, at my own expense, during this family's time of bereavement, I decided to visit with them to provide some spiritual and moral support. After all, they are my brothers and sisters within our faith community.

Besides unique interests and unique values, I also have some unique hobbies. They are (1) talking to people, (2) exercising daily, (3) listening to music, (4) developing and delivering speeches, and (5) serving as creative artists.

Talking to people. I thoroughly enjoy talking to people. I am excited to talk to people because I have this attitude that I never met any strangers. Nearly fifteen (15) months ago, I relocated from the State of Colorado to the State of Tennessee to live closer to my immediate family members. Although I am a new resident within this suburban community called the "Durham Farm Community," I now know everyone, and they know me. Hahaha! You see, I get a kick out of talking to anyone.

Exercise Daily. I have my exercise routine. I walk three (3) to five (5) miles daily. No. I do not lift weights. Rather, on the other hand, I do push-ups, sit-ups, and leg-ups. These daily exercises and walking help keep me in the best of health.

Listening to Music. I listen to all types of music: rhythm, blues, spirituals, gospel, classical, rap, rock and roll, hip-hop, and reggae. I listen to music as I drive my automobile, walk throughout my community, and listen at home. My life is music. Music is my life. Is not the music itself a kind of universal language?

Developing and delivering speeches. I get a thrill from developing and delivering speeches. However, I have been off my regular speaking circuit since the Covid pandemic. I have not been interested, therefore, in accepting speaking engagements. Nonetheless, as we adjust to dealing with COVID-19 through proper vaccination and other therapists, I am currently developing speeches about women in the Bible, which I plan to publish in a book on or before the conclusion of this year. After publishing these speeches, I will return to delivering speeches on my speaking circuit.

Serving as a Creative Artist. As stated before, I am employed as a businessman who is a creative artist. I am compensated for books, articles, presentations, etc., that I produce. My goal this year is to publish three (3) books. To achieve this goal, I write on an average of two thousand to three thousand words daily. These are some of the things that I do as a creative artist.

My unique personality includes some unique qualities. These qualities are (1) being a person with intuition, (2) being a good listener, (3) being a creative person, and (4) being a person of empathy. **Being a Person with Intuition**. Jewel Kilcher is a famous American female singer-songwriter. She wrote and performed a glorious song called "Intuition". Jewel sings, "Follow Your heart, Your Intuition; It will lead you in the right direction. Let go of Your mind, Your Intuition. It's easy to find. Just follow Your heart. Your Intuition."

Now, I am an extremely rational kind of man. In other words, given my level of education and training, I am an intelligent person. Nonetheless, I am also an intuitive kind of man. I can understand the feelings of my significant other without her telling or advising me specifically what she needs. Please believe me. I know how to read between the lines. You see, I have intuition. Hahaha!

Being a Good Listener. I know how to become

thoroughly engaged, especially in any meaningful relationship regarding love and romance. I have no problem turning off the telephone or television to provide that Special Woman my undivided attention. Hahaha! I am a good listener.

Being a Creative Person. I am a creative person. This is rather self-explanatory. I own and operate a business as a creative artist. I have demonstrated further my creativity by becoming a supporter and member of My Colombian Wife. Yes! Can you believe I paid the full membership fee to become a member? Hahaha!

Now, I am also fully cognizant that I have no guarantee that I will meet that Special Woman who is interested in my values, interests, hobbies, and qualities. This is the risk, nevertheless, that I am willing to take. I believe and know that the only thing that I need to fear is fear itself. I possess a unique personality.

Being a person of Empathy. The exciting writer and lawyer Robert Reich wrote an article about empathy in The Guardian. Robert Reich called his interesting and arresting article "Trump, Covid, and Empathy for the World's Least Empathetic Man." Reich criticizes the former twice-impeached President, Donald Trump, as the kind of person who is only concerned about himself and no one else. Do you know any people like that?

Chris Monaghan is a poet, songwriter, and musician from the City of Nashville. He may have been motivated by people like Donald Trump, who composed a wonderful song about empathy. Chris Monaghan entitled his song about empathy, "Through Your Eyes." "Through Your Eyes," If I could see the world through your eyes, Maybe

I'd understand why you do the things you do, Why you're always in a mood and speak with little lies If I could see through your eyes."

Last week, I visited with my devoted and loving mother in Memphis. It is roughly two hundred and fifty (250) miles from my home in Hendersonville. Now, most of us would do almost anything for our mother. Am I right about that? Well! My mother and I were seated at the dinner table eating dinner. I noticed suddenly that my mother's behavior had changed. She was not joking, acting, and being herself because she had become quiet. I saw her go in and out of consciousness. Immediately, I called the 911 hotline for an emergency ambulance to come and take my mother to the nearest hospital. My quick reaction was exactly what my mother needed.

Likewise, I want any available woman who is a member of my viewing and listening audience to understand this one thing about me. Namely, I am a person of empathy. Sometimes, I will ask God to help me walk in your shoes because I want to see things through your eyes. Hahaha!

MY FAVORITE PLACE
TO WRITE

In my new home, I have established a favorite place to write. But there exists one of two spots that I use for the purpose of writing. I jump off the traveling boat from the larger Aurora, Colorado, community to the smaller but fast-growing City of Hendersonville, Tennessee, community. I finally moved into the Lennar residential community called "Durham Farms." At that time, I needed to quickly establish my sense of belonging with a laser-like focus on becoming a more effective writer. To write, I intentionally established two (2) areas for writing: (1) my office and (2) my kitchen table island/living room area, which incidentally has become my favorite writing location.

When you enter my residence's front door, you are standing in a long, decorated hallway. In the distance, you see this seventy-five (75) inch Samsung Flatscreen staring and laughing. It is situated in the kitchen/living room section. Also, as you stand in the hallway, you see to your immediate left my office area. Four (4) cherry wood bookshelves are standing five (5) feet tall on the left-side and right-side lines of these white-colored walls. These bookshelves are stacked with a large variety of books. A tan-colored wooden tabletop and two (2) tan oak wood chairs are arranged between these cherry wood bookshelves in the middle of the floor. Whenever I sit here to write, I have this feeling of being uncomfortable, namely because my chair has no seat cushion. Well! I must purchase some padding for my office chair to feel more comfortable. (Hahaha) Nonetheless, I write here rarely and sparingly. But whenever I decide to write here, all I see are the bookshelves, my two (2) five (5) feet tan file cabinets, and high school and college graduation diplomas hanging from the wall. However, looking to the immediate left side of my office, I have only one window to look outside to notice the now ever-changing weather conditions. Sadly, whenever I sit here, I feel rather claustrophobic. In this writing environment, besides seeing books on the bookshelves, the only thing that catches my undivided attention is the gray siding of my next-door neighbor's house.

I do write, of course, in my kitchen/living room spot. It is a much larger open area with a much more scenic view. I regularly write from one of the four (4) comfortable high-back cushioned seated chairs. My writing pad, pencils, ink pens, and or the MacBook Pro Laptop Computer always accompany me.

Further, my view provides brighter scenery whenever I write at this location. Long story short, this writing spot is more pictorial, inspirational, and uplifting psychologically and spiritually. I am much closer to my talking 75-inch Samsung Flatscreen Television, the gray and black kitchen-colored appliances, the Samsung Refrigerator, the Frigidaire Upper and Lower Oven, the Frigidaire Microwave Oven, and other Frigidaire appliances. So, I can look through not just one (1) but five (5) different windows to see occasionally maybe the rainbow in the blue sky, the brown wooden porch swing, family pictures hanging around the four white walls, investigate my Master Bedroom and imagine how comfortable and irresistible it is to fall asleep in that King Size bed. Within my home, I am blessed to have two (2) places to write. They are my office area and the kitchen/living room area. My office location is where most of the books, resource information, and files are located. But it is smaller, confining, and less comfortable. The kitchen/living room area is more comfortable and less confining. It lets me hear my television talking occasionally, providing a more lively and brighter scenery.

A PLACE OF
CONNECTION

As an infant child and now as a mature adult, I continue to experience a special connection to the home of my fraternal grandparents, Robeia Saulsberry-Clayton and Saul Clayton, Sr. I make this declaration with great emotions as I am usually more stoical regarding revealing my true emotions. Nonetheless, I affectionately referred to them as Momma and Papa. Papa and Momma took seriously what the Bible says, "Be fruitful and multiply." They were parents of thirteen (13) children. When their children married, they had at least five or more children. For incidents, my parents had nine (9) children: four (4) daughters and five (5) sons.

Whenever I visited Momma and Papa's home, I had, besides my siblings, other children to play with and spend time with. Our days together were always pressure packed filled with fun and interesting games. Like Momma, Papa was deeply religious and spiritual, which aided them in being industrious and frugal. Papa exemplified a kind of Puritan mentality as reflected in his work habits. He supported his wife and family as a farmer who sold produce from his garden; and secured an additional income source.

From rural South Memphis, Tennessee to rural Northern Mississippi, Papa transported his adult children, older grandchildren, and other adults from the community to chop and pick cotton on this two-ton tarpaulin truck.

Momma remained, at home, to manage their household affairs, to care for, and supervise the grandchildren and other children in the neighborhood who also were left in her care. Papa and Momma agreed, because of the cancer of racism and discrimination in society, that she would never work outside their home. In contrast to Papa's level of sensitivity, particularly to his children and grandchildren, Momma was more heavy-handed with us. She was a stick discipliner who demonstrated "the no-no-sense mentality." She believed "spare the rod, spoils the child." Momma taught and instructed that the older children, the girls, and boys, had their own responsibilities. The older girls took care of the younger children. The older boys took care of the chores in the barn, but the older children worked in the garden together

The older girls, who included my oldest sister and female first cousins, ensured that the younger children were fed, their diapers changed, and assisted Momma in cleaning the house, cooking, and preparing the meals. On the other hand, the older boys, like me and my first male cousins, worked in the barn feeding the chickens, brought eggs from the chicken coop, retrieved meat from the smokehouse, slopped the hogs, and milked the cows.

My older sibling and first cousins, who were female and male, worked in the garden. We planted vegetable seeds, chopped the grass around the vegetables, and gathered the vegetables and fruits from the garden. Later in the fall or autumn, we canned the vegetables and fruits by storing them in containers.

Momma, Papa, and many of my older immediate and extended family members are now deceased. In 1975, as she was working in her garden, Momma died, at the age of 66, suddenly of a heatstroke. Papa lived to the ripe age of 108 years. Although he developed a self-imposed disease, my own beloved Father, Aaron (Otis) Clayton lived 78 years. May they all rest eternally within God's grace, blessings, mercy, and love!

Annually, the Robeia Saulsberry-Clayton and Saul Clayton Sr family members and dear friends gathered at their residence. We came together on the weekends of July 4th and Thanksgiving. These gatherings are family reunions in remembrance of the enduring legacy of Momma and Papa. Papa repeatedly said, "You all may not remember me, but Momma and I want our children, grandchildren, and relatives to know one another. We thank God for our family and friends." Certainly, I have fun memories of my fraternal grandparents' home. It serves as a mysterious reminder that God has brought my entire family and me far through hard work and tremendous sacrifice.

A FAMILIAR COLORADO LANDSCAPE

I enjoyed living in Aurora, Colorado. During my residence there, I obtained a spark not only for my many military veteran friends and their family members but also for the beautiful natural scenery of Colorado. Whenever I looked out of the master bedroom window or the back door of my patio area, I saw the snowcapped Colorado Rocky Mountains standing in the far distance. I sometimes thought, "If I could reach out and touch these snowcapped mountains, that would be a real miracle." Although I now live in Hendersonville, Tennessee, it is still rather difficult to erase from my memory the joy of seeing the natural beauty of Colorado.

Before driving to work in Denver or relaxing on the weekends, I arose in the early morning hours to run and walk through my suburban, rustic, and rural community. This exercise practice usually occurred during spring and summer, but due to the sudden, sometimes drastic weather changes during the Fall and Winter months, I was challenged to augment my workout pattern of walking/ running outdoors. At that time, I conducted my exercise regimen at the nearby Buckley Air Force Base Gym. The gym has an upstairs indoor track facility.

I must admit that running or jogging, weather permitting, was an emotional and spiritual high. I could see the beautiful Colorado skyline, the twisting and turning of the nature trails, and a few paved sidewalks. I lived in this unusual natural environment. Large portions of my community had wildlife like wild geese, foxes, hawks, and coyotes hanging around. I am sure, like all of us, these wild animals had this will somehow survive. Consequently, the local cattle ranchers, farmers, and my neighbors with pets were constantly mindful that they needed to always remain vigilant. It is a no-brainer. Animal predators care nothing about domestic animals or family pets.

When remembering how I navigated the natural terrain, sidewalks, and streets of my former Aurora community, something hit me like a ton of bricks. It is, namely, that the Hendersonville city streets and concert sidewalks are typically narrower than those in the City of Aurora. This may sound surprising, but "could it be that I solely miss seeing the beautiful Colorado landscape?"

THE IMPORTANCE OF THE WORD STRUGGLE

The word or term struggle resonates with me more than any other word. It speaks to my existence and the existence of every African American to work within American democracy toward being treated with dignity and respect. My people came to America, and were initially designated as indentured servants. In this capacity, African Americans were to work for their employer. Then, after completing their specific years of servitude, African Americans would be allowed to live as free human beings; but the White Americans who employed African Americans for indentured servitude changed the laws. African Americans subsequently were made slaves for life.

At that point, African Americans began their struggle for freedom, humanity, and dignity. This struggle began, however, long before Thomas Jefferson uttered these words, "We hold these truths that all men are created equal, and they are endowed by their creator with certain unenabled rights and among these are life, liberty, and the pursuit of happiness." Jefferson's words signaled a more indefatigable and intensive struggle for African Americans to fight for their freedom. This effort was reflected by Frederick Douglass and others who served in the Abolitionist Movement.

Now, I am interested in the Movement for Black Lives Matter (MBLM). This Movement is a continuation of what African Americans began long before the American Revolutionary War. It is best expressed by the word struggle. This is the reality that African Americans are willing to fight and even die so that they are treated as persons who are made in the image and likeness of God.

THIS MEMORY

I have this memory. My mother, Elizabeth Murphy Clayton, took me to get immunized for the first day of school. I was scheduled to begin at the neighborhood school, Geeter Elementary School. So, in preparation for school attendance, my mother and I boarded the Memphis City Bus to travel downtown to the John Gaston Hospital. It seems like it was only yesterday, which were the days of legal segregation and discrimination. At that time, the public water fountains were designated as White and Colored only drinking fountains.

While at the John Gaston Hospital, I received all kinds of vaccinations, which included shots for measles and mumps. There were no such things as anti-vaccination protests. Children's vaccinations were the law of the land since all school-aged children were to be vaccinated, and proof showed they had been vaccinated.

MY RECENT PROMPT TO REFLECT AND THINK

My family and friends are not as engaged as I am in this surprise "Happy Birthday "celebration for my mother, Elizabeth Murphy-Clayton. They have not been through the shared experiences with her as I have. It was that it was only yesterday. I remember that I had to prepare to begin elementary school. In preparation for my first day of school, my mother laboriously took the time, energy, and intestinal fortitude to teach me how to count from one to one hundred and how to learn to say the alphabet or the ABCs.

After we visited the John Gaston Hospital, my mother and I boarded the Memphis City Bus to ride home. It was late in the evening between 4 PM and 5 PM. Many employees from the various downtown places had gotten off their day jobs. Like us, they boarded the bus to travel home in the suburbs. My Mother and I were seated in the middle section of the bus. With each bus stop, I noticed that more and more people caused the bus to become overcrowded. Black bus riders had to get up to give it to the White passengers.

Long story short, my mother and I gave up our seats to a White man who sat alone. My mother stood up and held me in her arms. At that time, I was five years of age and the multiple vaccinations had gotten the best of me. I remember that these were the days of racial segregation and discrimination. I still have this memory.

MY ANCESTRY AND THE MOVEMENT FOR BLACK LIVES MATTER

Long before I could read or write, Silas Clayton, my fraternal grandfather, who we called Papa, recited the same story to me countless times every chance he got. Aaron Clayton, his grandfather was always the main character in Papa's story. This story encapsulates the Movement for Black Lives Matter (MBLM) long before anyone ever heard of this movement. it is correct to assert that Aaron Clayton and the MBLM saga began simultaneously as early as 1619, specifically when 20 African indentured servants arrived at Jamestown, Virginia. These Africans were undoubtedly the spiritual progenitors who provided a philosophical mindset set for their descendants from 1619 until today: striving for freedom as children of the creator.

Aaron was born a slave in Northern Mississippi or somewhere in South Carolina. He obtained his freedom as a teenager from slavery when Abraham Lincoln signed the Emancipation Proclamation, which freed all slaves from bondage to their white slave master. As a freedman, Aaron did not know where his parents and siblings or any other family members were. Here he was simply an illiterate slave with no family connection and nowhere to live or go. He wandered from one place to the next, trying to irk out an existence. At the end of his wandering existence, he obtained a job working along the mighty Mississippi River, loading, and unloading ships.

Aaron eventually married and fathered several children, specifically one son named Joe Rucker Clayton, who was Papa's father. Joe Rucker died, unfortunately, at an early death of what I do not know. I can only imagine his death could have been included in any number of things. No Black American had rights that any White American was duty-bound to respect. Who knows what my great grandfather, Joe Rucker, died of? The former slave, Aaron raised Silas like he was one of his sons. He raised him on his farm, which he had saved enough money to purchase. Aaron, the ex-slave, purchased nearly 200 areas of rich Northern Mississippi soil. Silas worked on the farm until his late teens or early twenties.

Aaron was married to the mother of Joe Rucker, who, like him, died prematurely. I do not recall her name. Aaron did remarry a woman called Ms. Alice. She was the local schoolteacher who taught Silas and the other black children in their rural Mississippi community in the local church building. Aaron was a member of the African Methodist Episcopal Church (AMEC), established and founded by Bishop Richard Allen. Allen and other African Americans broke away from the predominately white Methodist Episcopal Church (MEC). And, when they withdrew from MEC, Allen and his fellow believers took the name of AMEC. This church allowed and encouraged African

American members to exercise their Christian faith. This implies, laconically, for Richard Allen and Aaron Clayton, that religion, education, and freedom were all tied inextricably together.

Ms. Alice, like so many African Americans, is a person of mixed ancestry. The only picture of her and Aaron previously was provided by Papa. In this picture, Ms. Alice is a dark-skinned woman with distinctive Native American physical features. Of course, this is one of the reasons why I advised that although I am an African American, Elissa Washuta, who is of Native American descent, as people of color, we have much in common. Ms. Alice inspired and was a noble example for my grand aunt, Viola Clayton-Miller, to emulate. She majored in education at Rust College in Hollis Spring, Mississippi. Aunt Viola ultimately became entangled in and pursued a career as an educator in the North Mississippi Public Schools system.

Silas remained under Ms. Alice's tutelage from preschool through the sixth grade. At that time, there were no schools for Black children to attend beyond the sixth grade. To complete junior high school and high school, Silas relocated to Memphis to live with relatives and attend the Lemoyne Normal School. He only completed the seventh grade, later relocated to Saint Louis, Missouri, and worked several odd jobs there. Sometime thereafter, Aaron became severely ill and later died. Aaron left his children and grandchildren approximately 200 acres of land at his death. This truly was an amazing and extraordinary accomplishment for an uneducated former slave. Silas returned home to Northern Mississippi to care for the family and work on and manage the Aaron Clayton family farm.

A LETTER TO MY MOMMA FROM THE MAYOR OF THE CITY OF HENDERSONVILLE

Today, I obtained a letter from the Mayor of Hendersonville. I made this request of him because of my love for my devoted mother. But as I thought more about it, I realized the mayor possibly cared less about my mother's upcoming surprise birthday celebration. It is because she does not reside or vote in Hendersonville. Essentially, the Mayor's job is to focus on the city residents' social well-being, such as making sure crime is not an issue. And that the city streets are clean and there are no holes in the streets.

I obtained a full gasoline tank for my car before traveling to Memphis. I was going to Memphis to pick up my mother and one of my sisters, Faye, and transport them to my home in Hendersonville. However, to get the needed automobile gasoline, I gassed up at the local Sam Wholesale Store, approximately two and a half miles from my residence. Filling my car's gas tank costs nearly fifteen dollars.

Elizabeth Murphy Clayton has demonstrated without

question that she is a smart, independent kind of woman and mother. For domestic reasons, she separated and divorced my father, Aaron (Otis) Clayton. In the process, she raised their nine children: four daughters and five sons. My mother achieved this tremendous task as a single parent. All her nine children completed high school. Her five sons reflect and embody Elizabeth's American patriotic attitude. They served with honor, distinction, and "For God and Country" in the United States Armed Forces.

HAPPY BIRTHDAY CELEBRATION FOR MY MOMMA

My family and friends are not as engaged as I am in this upcoming surprise "Happy Birthday "celebration for my mom, Elizabeth Murphy-Clayton. They have not been through the shared experiences with her as I have. It appears that it was only yesterday. I remember that I had to prepare to begin elementary school. In preparation for my first day of school, Momma laboriously took the time and energy and had the intestinal fortitude to teach me how to count from one to one hundred and learn to say the alphabet or the ABCs.

I am joyous about my mother's upcoming 86th birthday celebration. I remain thankful and grateful that I still have her here. It is because, throughout my entire life, she has been a major source of inspiration and motivation. When other persons have often tried to discourage me from serving in the United States Army, my Momma advised me that service to God and Country is the highest honor for any true American patriotism.

I remember on endless occasions that Momma worked three different jobs to provide for me, my sisters, and my brothers. She and Aaron, my father, together had nine children: four daughters and five sons in their marriage. However, since they experienced some troubling domestic issues, Momma eventually decided to separate and later divorced Aaron. From then on, my siblings and I were raised mostly by Momma as a single parent. In all honesty, we lived at times a kind of penury existence. No matter how difficult things were within her household, Momma always kept and maintained her faith. She was always a hard-working woman and mother who believed with pure determination and grit that God would help her to make a way out of no way.

Theologians and womanist theologians know James Cones as the Father of African American Theology. Cone is the first African American Theologian to write a systematic treatise called *Black Theology and Black Power*, which reveals the impact of the black power movement and Malcolm X on Cone's thinking. He additionally authored *The Spirituals and the Blues: An Interpretation*, and in this insightful publication Cone insists that the blues are sacralized spirituals. Cone's theological assertion makes perfect sense when considering my Momma's spirituality. I often recalled hearing Momma sing about "God's Amazing Grace," then, sometime thereafter, I could hear her sing a classic B.B. King's blues song, "The Thrill is Gone. My Baby has left me, and I feel so all alone." The spirituals and the blues are the same size as the coin. We cannot have one without the other.

Momma is now in the early stage of crippling Alzheimer's disease, which sadly reveals that, physically and mentally, she is not the woman she once was. Her condition is a reminder that life is itself extremely short. So, as we are concerned about Momma's total well-being, my sibling and I meet periodically among ourselves. We have concluded basically in our meetings that, although she may outlive us, our Momma will not die in a nursing home. We have made this possible through health and medical insurance to have a nurse and physical therapist to provide her in-home care. We additionally take shifts to be with Momma 24 hours and seven days weekly.

MY BELOVED FATHER'S CONFESSION TO MY DEVOTED MOMMA: QUEEN ELIZABETH

I am a clergyman, a Baptist preacher, and a product of the African American Church tradition experience, a church with a history of being socially, economically, and politically engaged. Martin Luther King Jr's life and legacy reflect and exemplify the clergy's role in the African American Church. Mindful of this heritage regardless of where I live, I consciously try to establish relationships with elected and pivotal public leaders.

I obtained letters for my Momma's upcoming birthday from public officials in the City of Hendersonville. These were letters from the Honorable Mayor of Hendersonville and the Chief of Police. I made this request of them because of my abiding love, respect, and devotion for my devoted Mother. But, as I thought about it, the Mayor could possibly say less about my Momma's upcoming surprise birthday. It is because she does not reside or vote in Hendersonville. Essentially, in contrast to writing a letter to a nonresident, the mayor's primary job is to focus on the social well-being of his city residents, such as making sure crime is not an issue. And, he must ensure that the city streets are cleaned and that there are no potholes.

Well! I obtained letters from both the distinguished Mayor and the Chief of Police. In his letter, the mayor states, "Thank you for celebrating your birthday in Hendersonville today (even if you didn't know that you would be celebrating your birthday today). I have gathered that you should be very proud of your accomplishments, especially your children and their children. I am raising only two children. I cannot imagine raising nine." The Chief of Police remarks, "The celebrating of one's Mother, is very near and dear to my heart. I fondly cherish the memories of my own mother. She was tremendously important to me, and I still take actions, to this day, to honor her memory and legacy, and will continue to do so!"

I obtained a full tank of gasoline for my fashionable four-door Red Cajun Chevrolet Impala before I jetted away to Memphis. I needed gasoline to drive nearly two hundred and fifty miles to Memphis to pick up Momma, one of my sisters, Faye Clayton-Baker, and immediately made an about-face to transport them back to my home here in Hendersonville. I was delighted to have Faye spend quality time with me and Momma. In years of age, I am approximately three years older than Faye. Long story short, Faye helped and assisted me as we cared for Momma. Since Faye and Momma had never seen nor visited my Hendersonville home, they were anxious to offer suggestions and insight into how I needed to beautify my bachelor pad.

To get the needed automobile gasoline, I gassed up at

the local Sam Wholesale Store, approximately two- and one-half miles from my bachelor pad. Filling my car gas tank cost nearly fifteen dollars, allowing me to drive to nearly two hundred and fifty miles to reprieve Momma and Faye.

Elizabeth Murphy-Clayton has demonstrated without question that she is a smart, resilient, independent kind of woman and mother. She became a young mother at the tender age of fifteen. From age 15 to age 25, she gave birth to nine children. Therefore, during these years of child birthing, she temporarily dropped out of high school. Momma believed nevertheless in the power of quality education as she always insisted that quality education could transform and improve the well-being of any individual. Although she worked during the day and sometimes on weekends, Momma attended night school to earn her diploma at the Booker T. Washington High School evening school.

Again and again, for troubling and trying domestic reasons, Momma made the difficult decision to separate and divorce my father, Aaron. I cannot emphasize this fact enough. In the process, she raised me and my siblings as a single parent, which is clearly a tremendous and monumental accomplishment. I take my hat off to my Momma throughout eternity because of what she was able to achieve. She walked the walk and talked the talk. My Momma was taught by a marvelous and moral example, which inspired me, my sisters, and my brothers, to complete high school and pursue higher levels of education. Further, her five sons reflect and embody my Momma's patriotic American attitude. They unselfishly served with honor, distinction, "For God and Country" as soldiers in the United States Armed Forces. My delightful Momma is without question the matriarch of our family, and her birthday remains a joyous celebration for my siblings, other extended family members, and dear friends. Interestingly, before my father's death, he said to my Momma, "Elizabeth, I want to thank you for keeping our family together."

"YOU GOING TO BE JUST LIKE YOUR FATHER"

Ethel Ray Murphy was my maternal step-grandmother. She married my maternal grandfather, Luther Murphy, Sr, sometime after the untimely death of my grandmother, Rebecca Murphy. Ethel preferred that her stepchildren and grandchildren call her "Little Momma." Well! Little Momma never birthed biologically any children. Before marrying Luther, Little Momma had been involved in an abusive marriage relationship. She had subsequently had several miscarriages. However, Little Momma raised my youngest uncle Eugene, as her child from infancy to adulthood. Eugene incidentally is one year my senior. Little Momma was certainly a highly talented and multitalented woman. She operated her own cosmetology business from home, played the piano and the organ, and served as a musician for several local churches. She and Grandfather Luther were devoted Christians. But, while Luther was committed to the Baptist tradition, Little Momma was orientated to the holy Pentecostal tradition, namely the Church of God in Christ.

Little Momma ran her household and everyone who occasioned her presence. In short, she was a strict disciplinarian who believed that "spare the rod spoil the child." Whenever she decided to discipline me, I would never cry or exhibit any sense of pain. I reacted to her whipping constantly in a stoic like demeanor. My behavior irritated Little Momma endlessly. And, to strike fear into my entire existence, she would say, "you are so hard-headed. I am going to tell Luther on you."

Now, Grandfather Luther believed without hesitation anything Little Momma said. If she said the sky was green, and it was blue, Luther believed that was the gospel truth. For the most part, he was a no-nonsense disciplinarian who was more like a slaver master. Child abuse was pure idiocy to him. Grandfather Luther sometimes whipped or beat his children or grandchildren with an extension cord.

I recalled one thing as if it was yesterday. It was a despairing remark Little Momma made to me. She stated, "You are going to be just like your father." Little Momma's remark has always haunted me, like a ghost, even to this day. My hard-working father was named Aaron (or Otis) Clayton. Believe me. Explaining my father's name Aaron is another interesting story of its own. He changed his name from Otis to Aaron when he finally, as a grown man, viewed a copy his birth certificate. When my father was born in rural Northern Mississippi, African Americans did not typically have access to a physician. The local midwife delivered infant babies born to Black women.

Since the midwife knew my father's grandfather, Aaron, she wrote Aaron on his birth certificate. However, my fraternal grandparents, Rebecca, and Silas Sr, vehemently insisted that, at birth, they named my father Otis. In all candor and honesty, he did his best to honor the name Otis for most of his adult life. But, when he saw the name Aaron on the birth certificate, my father legally changed his name from Otis to Aaron. Silas Sr, or Papa as we called him affectionately made this joke with my father: "You missed up the name Otis. I guess you are now going to miss up the name Aaron."

My parents, Aaron and Elizabeth, were married on paper for nearly seventeen years. They had nine children during their marriage: five boys and four daughters. When they married, Aaron was eighteen, and Elizabeth was nearly fifteen. Therefore, because of their agrarian lifestyle, their youth, and their culture of systematic racism, they never completed their high school education. While my mother eventually did complete the eleventh grade, my father obtained only seven years of formal education. I remember him working various jobs trying tirelessly to support my mother, his children, and their household.

I am his oldest son, and my father often confided in me when he came home in the evening after work. He talked about his daily experiences. Maybe he did this because he called me the nickname Puddin. As we usually watched religiously the evening news, he spoke to me about his anxieties, frustrations, and how he coped daily with racism and discrimination specifically with his employer.

He once worked in Memphis as a common laborer for the non-unionized Navy Yard Cotton Compressed Company. This was an employer, like most businesses in the deep South, who believed Black employees had no rights white people needed to respect. Therefore, white employees worked, no matter their level of experience or competency, as leaders over their more skilled and knowledgeable Black employees. On many occasions, my father commented, "I trained this young white male teenager in the duties, responsibilities, and obligations of employment. But, Navy Yard Cotton Compressed Company management promoted this young teenager to my supervisor. And, since he was the supervisor within my area of responsibility, this young teenager wanted me to say "Yes Sir and No Sir. This is so dehumanizing and disrespectful. I do not know how long I can take this."

Sadly, to make ends meet and to provide for his family, my father decided to generate other sources of income. Besides employment at the Navy Yard Compressed Company, he became his own employer. Aaron began to bootleg, sell corn whiskey, and become a gambler. Unfortunately, my father's effort to produce additional income took a toll on my parent's marriage relationship. He was arrested several times for bootlegging whiskey from Mississippi into Tennessee. He was also arrested for selling bootleg whiskey from his home. Because of his home's booming bootlegging business, the Memphis/Shelby County Police entered our home with arrest warrants. On one occasion, the police found five gallons of illegal corn whiskey. However, since my father was not home, the police arrested my mother, which is the only time in her life that she was ever arrested.

A few years later, my parents separated and eventually divorced. My Father relocated to Saginaw, Michigan for a better quality of life. He became an employee of the General

Motors Corporation (GMC), where he ultimately retired. His job at GMC was union-organized and provided higher wages and better working conditions, including medical benefits for employees and their family members., when he relocated to Saginaw, my father repeatedly asked my mother to move there with his children. He believed there that his wife and their children would enjoy a better quality of life. However, my mother rejected his offer. She remarked, "we did not make it in Memphis, Tennessee. I do not believe we can make it in Saginaw, Michigan."

My father, Aaron (or Otis) was not a highly educated man, but he was, in many respects, truly a wise man who deeply loved his family and enjoyed an abiding relationship with God. He did the best he could to provide and care for his family. But, for him, the old South was a dead-end street with no exist. He wanted my mother and their children to move with him to the North. Overall, based on his experience, he understood that the North afforded a much better environment. While living there, he purchased him a lovely home and owned several rental properties. He was never a devoted churchman. But he believed and had faith in God. On the weekends, my father cooked meals at his home and invited relatives and friends to drop by for breakfast, dinner, and drinks. He would also invite homeless persons into his home for free meals. I saw him countlessly give complete strangers food and money, and he sent them on their way.

I am a clergyman and Baptist preacher with years of experience in pulpit ministry. Whenever I visited Saginaw to preach to friends who were Senior Pastors of various local congregations, my father always found a way to be present to lend his support. He did not talk about his faith in God. Rather, my father put in his faith into action. Like the New Testament writer, he believed faith without works is dead. Ethel Ray Murphy, known as Little Momma One, said something to me. I now believe it is true. "You are going to be just like your father".

REFLECTIONS ABOUT A COURAGEOUS WOMAN

My family and friends are not as engaged as I am in this upcoming surprise "Happy Birthday "celebration for my mom, Elizabeth Murphy-Clayton. They have not been through the shared experiences with her as I have. It appears that it was only yesterday. I remember that I had to prepare to begin elementary school. In preparation for my first day of school, Momma laboriously took the time and energy and had the intestinal fortitude to teach me how to count from one to one hundred and how to learn to say the alphabet or the ABCs.

I am joyous about my mother's upcoming 86th birthday celebration I remain thankful and grateful that I still have her here. It is because throughout my entire life she has been a major source of inspiration and motivation. When other persons have often tried to discourage me from serving in the United States Army, my Momma advised me that service to God and Country is the highest honor for any true American patriot1c.

I remember on endless occasions that Momma worked three different jobs to provide for me, my sisters, and my brothers. She and Aaron, my father, together had nine children: four daughters and five sons in their marriage. However, since they experienced some troubling domestic issues, Momma eventually decided to separate and later divorced Aaron. From that point forward, my siblings and I were raised mostly by Momma as a single parent. In all honesty, we lived at times a kind of penury existence. No matter how difficult things were within her household, Momma always kept and maintained her faith. She was always a hard-working woman and mother who believed with determination and grit that God would help her make a way out of no way.

Theologians and womanist theologians know James Cones as the Father of African American Theology. Cone is the first African American Theologian to write a systematic treatise called *Black Theology and Black Power*, which reveals the impact of the black power movement and Malcolm X on Cone's thinking. He also authored The Spirituals and the Blues: An Interpretation, and in this insightful publication, Cone insists that the blues are simply sacralized spirituals. Cone's theological assertion makes perfect sense when I think about my Momma's spirituality. I often recalled hearing Momma sing about "God's Amazing Grace," and then sometime thereafter, I could hear her sing a classic B.B. King's blues song, "The Thrill is Gone. My Baby has left me, and I feel so all alone." The spirituals and the blues are the same size as the coin. We cannot have one without the other.

Momma is now in the early stage of crippling Alzheimer's disease, which sadly reveals that, physically and mentally, she is not the woman she once was. Her condition is a reminder that life is itself extremely short. So, as we are concerned about Momma's total well-being, my sibling and I meet periodically among ourselves. We have concluded basically in our meetings that, although she may outlive us, our Momma will not die in a nursing home. We have made this possible through health and medical insurance to have a nurse and physical therapist to provide her in-home care. We additionally take shifts to be with Momma 24 hours and seven days weekly.

Poems

AT MY MOMMA'S DINNER TABLE

Morning time. At my Momma's dinner table, I see old family pictures lining the wall, furniture neatly assigned and aligned

I hear the silence of sound echoing in
Momma talks
Prayer talks
God talks

Suddenly, God's presence is evident
Is evident in bright sunshine
Is evident in birds singing
Is evident in being who I am

I hear unrevealed stories about Dad who's deceased, yet alive in these maturing days.

Evening time. My Momma dinner table.

JUST A VESSEL OF THE WORD MADE FLESH

Oh Yes! The word has been made flesh
It's mind
It's body
It's soul

Does the preacher really, really, really know the word made flesh?
She preaches it.
She prays it.
She sings it.
She moves within it.

Oh Yes! God speaks throughout eternity.
The word made flesh.
The word made flesh in agape love

MY DAILY PRAYER

Oh God! Oh God! Oh God! I hear you loud and crystal clear to
Somehow love your creation, even the murderer, even the
rapist, and even our neighbor.

Now, Guns daily shoot the innocent
Innocent children
Innocent women
Innocent men

But I seek too
Visit those in prison
Feed the hungry
Give ease to troubling minds
Become an example of your mercy, your grace, and your love.

Oh God! Oh God! Oh God! I daily give you thanks. Glory
Hallelujah! Glory Hallelujah! Glory Hallelujah.

Sermons

LUKE 1:30-32A, AND 2:7
Achieving the Impossible

Our birth in the ghetto provides no limitation on the great things we can accomplish today, tomorrow, or in the future. Some people think that where we are born can casts a dark cloud over our head. Other people have this negative attitude that we can never become all that can become, and that we are unable to say Yes, we can. We must believe, however, that through God's love, grace, and power, we can achieve the impossible. Brother Matthews states, "With humans it is impossible, but with God, all things are possible" (Matthew 19:26). President Barack Obama says, therefore, without hesitation and equivocation, "Yes. We Can. Yes. We can."

Please allow me to explain basically and biblically the reason why we can go from being born in any ghetto to becoming great through our various fields of endeavor. Yes! Through God's power, we can become great wherever we are. The ghetto is a place where there exit substandard schools, exists inadequate health care, exists bad nutrition, exists liquors stores on every street corner, exists low-class hotels, exists police brutality, exists streets gangs, exists of pimps, players, and prostitutes exist a negative-minded set, exists no place to call home, exists the red line district, and exists where the railroad tract marks off the boundary. Well! This is what we call the ghetto. Has anyone here been born in the ghetto? Has anyone here ever said that you were not going to make it?

Well! Jesus is Emmanuel or God with us, the Lamb of God who takes upon our sins, healed the sick, raised the dead, was a friend to the friendless, was a father to the fatherless, was a Mother to the motherless, and gave ease to trembling to minds, was nailed to the Cross on a hill called Calvary. And this same Jesus is alive because he lives with my mind, heart, and soul.

But did you know that Jesus was born in the ghetto? This is exactly where the manager was. It is a place located in the ghetto. Dr. Larry George is an outstanding Hebrew Bible Scholar who wrote his Ph.D. dissertation— four (400) hundred pages about the 21st Chapter of John's Gospel. Professor George has visited the Middle East several times and the historic City of Bethlehem. He insists that the manager where Jesus was born is-- for the lack of a better word is nothing but-- a ghetto.

The manager is a cave where animals like sheep, donkeys, and cows are there to eat food and the manager also protects them from the winds, rains, storms, and other elements. Additionally, whenever there are sheep, cows, and other animals, there will also be animal dropping were roaches, rats, and other insects appear. However, the manager is the ghetto where Jesus was born.

Brother Danny Hathaway wrote his famous song called "Little Ghetto Boy." "Little ghetto boy, playing in the street; whatcha gonna do when you grow up; and have to face responsibility? Will you spend your days and nights in the pool room? Will you sell caps of madness to the neighborhood? Little ghetto boy, Little ghetto boy."

Now! Despite being born in the ghetto, Jesus matriculated from the ghetto to become great because he made a difference in the world. But what is meant by the concept of greatest? It means, among other things, doing things extensively to the best of our ability, working tirelessly to make a difference, and having the no-nonsense attitude that dangerous excessive altruism is never enough. Yes! This is what Jesus did with his life. He transitions from being born in a dark, dim ghetto to demonstrating and illustrating the greatest.

Listen! The gospel writer—Luke--says, "The angel said to (Mary), "Do not be afraid, Mary, for you have found favor with God. And behold, you will be conceived in your womb, bring forth a Son, and call His name Jesus. He will be great." "And Mary brought forth her firstborn Son, and wrapped him in swaddling clothes, and laid Him in a manger because there was no room for them in the inn" (Luke 1:30-32, 2:7). This manger was the ghetto. Yes! Let us note ways Jesus goes from being born in the ghetto to accomplish some great things.

Note! Jesus goes from being born in the ghetto to becoming great because he spent his life fighting against ignorance. Jesus learned from the school of hard knock, taught his family members, and taught his disciples. He had no problem being taught and teaching others. But what do we mean by this concept of ignorance? Simply put, it refers to "the state or fact of being ignorant, lack of knowledge, education or awareness."

Brother Donald Trump is a classic case of what it means to be ignorant. Trump presently serves as the President of the United States of America. No. I did not vote for him, but he is still our President. Now! I do not hate Trump and neither do I want anything unfortunate to happen to him or his family. I love this Brother. However, like some of you, I despise his policies and practices because they are designed ultimately to hurt poor people who are Black, White, and oppressed people across religion, race, and ethnic lines.

Brother Trump is, nevertheless, one of the most uninformed President we have ever had in American History. Despite what our intelligence agencies officials say, he insists that He insists that the Russian government did not interfere with our recent Presidential election. He refuses to consult with his top general, other military leaders, and national security leaders regarding what is best for America. Yes! We can conclude our Brother, Donald Trump, is not as intelligent as he should be.

Jesus fought, however, against all kinds of ignorance. First, Jesus learned from the school of hard knocks. Next, he taught his family members; and finally, Jesus taught disciples. Brother Luke—the gospel writer-- insists that Jesus grew in wisdom, knowledge and understanding. Therefore, Jesus spent eighteen or more years living in Egypt (Matthew 2:13-23); and while living in Egypt, Jesus studied undoubtedly philosophy as well as theology with various philosophers, professors, and rabbis. Jesus grew in wisdom, knowledge, and understanding (Luke 2:39-40). Additionally, Jesus taught his family members. They did not understand his purpose for living so he taught Mary, his Mother, Joseph—his Father, and other family members. Jesus told them, "I must be about my Father's business (Luke 2:39-52).

Jesus taught his disciples The Beatitudes, "Blessed are the poor in spirit, for theirs is the kingdom of heaven; Blessed are the meek, for they shall inherit the earth. . . Blessed are those who are persecuted for righteousness' sake, for there is the kingdom of heaven. Rejoice and be exceedingly glad, for great is your reward in heaven" (Matthew 5:1-12).

Yes! Jesus spends productive time in fighting against ignorance. So,

what does this suggest to us? Like Jesus, we must all must develop the ability to not only preach. Also, we must prepare ourselves to become effective teachers of the gospel of Christ. Brother Paul argues, "Study to show ourselves approved that a workman need not be ashamed but rightfully dividing the word of truth (2 Timothy 2;15).

Listen! Brother Luke--says, "The angel said to (Mary), "Do not be afraid, Mary, for you have found favor with God. And behold, you will be conceived in your womb, bring forth a Son, and call His name Jesus. He will be great." "And Mary brought forth her firstborn Son, and wrapped him in swaddling clothes, and laid Him in a manger, because there was no room for them in the inn" (Luke 1:30-32, 2:7).

Jesus, our Lord, was born in the ghetto. Consequently, some people counted him out saying, "Can anything come out of Nazareth? (John 1:46). Nevertheless, Jesus did not allow the negative things that people said to him and about him get him to bog him down. He focused on what God called him to do and not what he wanted to do. Repeatedly, he stated, "Not my will but thine will be done" (Luke 23:42). Jesus was called by God basically to love all people regardless of their race, religion creed, and color. Yes! Jesus—our Lord--fought ignorance and became great within human history.

Note! **Jesus goes from being born in the ghetto to become great because he healed those who were in need.** Jesus healed at least in two ways. First, Jesus healed people externally; and he healed people internally. Jesus healed people externally because he touched them, and they touched him (Luke 6:17-19).

Let me tell you this story. For more than twelve years-- this Sister-- let me call her Sister Ann had her monthly cycle. For some reason, her monthly cycle would not go away. So, Sister Ann went to this doctor and that doctor for any medical cure. And, in the process, she spent all her money. But, somehow and someway, Sister Ann makes her way to Jesus. And Jesus heals her of affliction and sickness, which she had been suffering. Then, Jesus tells Sister Ann, "Your faith has made you whole (Luke 8:43-48; Mark 5:23-34; Matthew 9:18-26).

May I tell you a secret! Jesus is still in the healing business. Sometimes, our God heals us through other people. God uses our doctors sometimes through surgery to heal us. Sister Topeka Sam and Brother Fred Clay come quickly to mind. Sister Topeka was arrested and thrown in jail for a nonviolent crime. After she got out of prison, God blessed, enabled, and empowered Topeka to develop a powerful ministry called The Ladies of Hope. When women are released from jail, Sister Topeka's ministry works endlessly to help Women readjust to life. Jesus is still in the healing business.

At the tender age of seventeen, Brother Clay was arrested unjustly and remained in prison for thirty-eight (38) years for a crime that he did not commit. Though African American man in prison, his family stopped visiting him. But Brother Clay was introduced—to this local church prison ministry—where he met Brother Doran Dibble and his loving family. Moreover, Brother Dibble- which is not important- is a European American, and he is also employed as a software engineer. Brother Dibble volunteered to visit Brother Clay in prison. Subsequently, Brother Clay greatly impacted Brother Dibble's deep Christian devotion and commitment. Then, Brother--Dibble began to bring his wife and children to visit Brother Clay. In the process, they visited him for nearly twenty years driving two to three hours in each direction. Brother Dibble's church also pursued this team of Lawyer's with the Innocent Project to take Brother Fred Clay's case to court. Finally, the Innocent Project convinced the judge to overturn Brother Clay's unjust prison conviction. After spending nearly 40ty years in prison, Brother Fred Clay is a free man.

Yes! Jesus is still in the healing. The Lord may not come when you want God to show up. God always shows up right on time. And when God shows up in our lives, God shows out.

Yes! Sister Mary gave birth to Jesus in a ghetto of Bethlehem. There was "no room for them in the inn." And, no one there in the City of Bethlehem extended any form of hospitality to them. Therefore, Jesus was born in a manger, which was right in the ghetto. Despite this, Jesus was able, with the help of Almighty God, to go from the ghetto to greatness. He healed the sick and the afflicted.

Yes! Like Jesus Christ—our Lord--We have work to do. Regardless of our chosen field of endeavor, we have work to do. We can go—with God's love, power, and grace- from being born in the ghetto to obtain greatness now henceforth and forever more. Yes! We can go from the ghetto to achieve greatness.

Note! Jesus goes from being born in the ghetto to becoming great because he preached the gospel's good news. What is the difference between bad news and good news?" The bad news is that Tennessee Governor Bill Haslam may not grant Sister Cynthia Brown clemency before he leaves his office. The bad news is the news that recently, our dear Friend and Brother, Attorney Quentin White, died from complications with cancer. The Bad news is that General James Mattis resigned-- as the Secretary of Defense.

The good news is the news that Brother Kenneth Thomas recorded a video dancing for his infant son, who was fighting leukemia at the Children's Hospital, and his son is now cancer-free. The good news is that an elderly man—before he died—purchased 14 Christmas gifts for his next-door neighbor's small daughter. The good news is the news that a Young girl—whom I will call Sister Sue— suffered from an inoperable brain tumor, but her tumor disappeared, and her doctors do not have an explanation. This is good news.

Now, what is the good news of the gospel that Jesus preached? Jesus preached, "The Spirit of the Lord is upon Me Because God has anointed Me to preach the gospel to the poor; God has sent Me to heal the brokenhearted, to proclaim liberty to the captives to set at liberty those who are oppressed; To proclaim the acceptable year of the Lord" (Luke 4: 18-19).

Jesus preached that the Kingdom of God is at hand. In other words, no matter how bad things happen to us, we have the assurance that God is in charge and in control of this world. Yes! Regardless, of what Trump says, Putin says and anyone else says, God always has the first and the last word.

Reverend Bernice Long preached a powerful sermon. Her sermon text came from Isiah Chapter 9 verse 6. She called her sermon, "Do You Know Jesus?" and her question. This is an important question for all of us. She does not ask whether our Mamma, Daddy, Sister, Brother, Neighbor or anyone else knows Jesus. More importantly, she asks the question "Do You Know Jesus?"

Yes! I know Jesus for myself. Jesus was born in the ghetto in the City of Bethlehem. And their people who counted him out. They said that undoubtedly, he was not going to make it. But Jesus kept on fighting against ignorance. Jesus kept on healing people of their sickness. Jesus kept on preaching the gospel of the good news that God is able and God is in charge.

Oh! Yes! I know Jesus for myself. He touched me and made me whole. And I can hear Jesus singing the words of this song, "To Be Young Gifted and Black."

To Be young, gifted and Black
Oh what a lovely precious dream
To Be young, gifted and Black
Open your heart to what I mean

You know in this whole world
There are billions of boys and girls
Who are young, gifted, and Black
And that's a fact.

To Be Young, gifted, and Black
We must begin to tell our young
There's a whole world waiting for you
This is quest has just begun

When you feel really low
Yeah. There's a great truth you should know
When you're young, gifted, and Black
Your soul's intact

To Be young gifted and Black
Young, gifted, and Black
How I long to know the truth
There are times when I look Back
And I am haunted by my youth

Oh! My joy today
Is that we can all be proud to say
To Be young, gifted, and Black
And it is show nough where it is at.
I don't think you believe me.

We may have been born in the ghetto; but through
the love, power, and grace of God, we can achieve the
impossible. We can go from living in any dark and dim
ghetto to achieving greatness.

LUKE 4:18-19

From the Ghetto to Greatness

I want to preach this morning on the subject, "From the Ghetto to Greatness." I want to read from the Gospel of Luke Chapter 4, verses 18 through 19. I am reading from the New King James translation of scripture. Jesus says, "The Spirit of the Lord is upon Me. Because (God) has anointed Me To preach the gospel to the poor: God has sent Me to heal the brokenhearted". To proclaim liberty to the captives, And recovery of sight to the blind, To set at Liberty those who are oppressed; To proclaim the acceptable year of the Lord".

Donny Hathaway was a prevalent rhythm, blues, and gospel singer. He had a wonderful song called "Little Ghetto Boy".

Little ghetto boy
Playing in the ghetto street
What'cha gonna do when you grow up
And have to face responsibility?
Will you spend your days and nights in a pool room?
Will you sell caps of madness to the neighborhood?
Little ghetto boy

You already know how rough life can be
'Cause you've seen so much pain and misery
Little ghetto boy
Your daddy was blown away
He robbed that grocery store
Don't you know that was a sad, sad old day?
All of your young life
You've seen such misery and pain
The world is a cruel place
And it ain't gonna change
You're so young
And you've got so far to go
But I don't think you'll reach your goal, young man
Hanging by the pool room door
Look out, son

The famous and iconic Lebron James was born in the ghetto. He was a ghetto boy. His single-parent Mother raised him. They lived in an impoverished community in Akron, Ohio. Gloria James, Lebron's mother, gave birth to him at the tender age of sixteen. Gloria James did her best to be the best Mother that she could. Meanwhile, Lebron was exposed to athletics and basketball at a young age. In the process, he demonstrated that he possessed God-given talents, ability, and determination. He became an exceptional basketball player. Lebron James has accomplished something no other basketball player has ever done. He graduated high school as the best player in the nation and was drafted as the top player into the National Basketball Association (NBA). Lebron James has spent twenty years playing professional basketball at the highest level.

He has become the highest scorer in NBA history and one of the all-time greatest basketball players. Lebron James is now worth a billion dollars. But, most importantly, he has taken and given enormous amounts of money to build a school to help underprivileged children obtain a quality education. He is a classic case of going from the ghetto to greatness.

Now, Lebron James and Jesus have something in common. Jesus was born in a barn in the City of Bethlehem. It was an impoverished area where animals and other livestock lived. This was the ghetto. Jesus and his family could not lay their heads in a comfortable environment. Jesus was born in the ghetto.

But the ghetto is not necessarily a physical location. We can be in the ghetto by thinking negative thoughts, doing negative things to ourselves, and doing harmful things to others. The ghetto is both a physical and mental experience.

Most importantly, this text suggests how we can go from the ghetto to greatness. **First, to go from ghetto to greatness, we must have a virtual faith in tough times.** When you are going from the ghetto greatness, you will experience a broken heart. Who among us has not had a broken heart? We have all faced a broken heart. We sometimes face broken hearts in our marriage relationship.

But let me be crystal clear. I know what I am talking about. I did not get married to get a divorce in the judgment hall of divorce court. Anytime you go through a divorce, you will experience a broken heart. Divorce and a broken heart go together. Now, some of us have faced broken hearts with our children. Some of our children have gone the wrong way. They have become prodigal sons and daughters. Oh

Yes, experiencing the death of a family member or friend is going through a broken heart. Death is the final common denominator for all of us. Death is the great equalizer.

Now, the ghetto is not just a physical location. The ghetto is also a mental location, but if we go from the ghetto to greatness, We must have a virtual faith in God. Our faith in God will help us deal with tough times. Our faith in God helps us to believe that God is in control of this world. Our faith in God allows us to believe that we have an eternal moral purpose in light of which a thousand years are as yesterday when it is past as a watch in the night. Going from the ghetto to greatness, we need faith in tough times.

Next, to go from the ghetto to greatness, we must preach the deliverance by preaching the deliverance of the captives. I want you to know that we are all captives of something. And what I am captive of, you may not be a captive of that. But, we are all captive by something.

Yasef Salaam was a captive in prison. He was wrongly incarcerated for a crime he did not commit. Donald Trump insisted that Yasef and his other six friends receive the death penalty. Salaam and his friends remained imprisoned for seven years but were later acquitted. Yasef Salaam and his friends were incarcerated for a crime they did not commit. While Yasef and his friends were in prison, someone preached deliverance to them.

More than ever before, the church must preach about deliverance. The white church and the black church must preach deliverance. The Southern Baptist Convention excommunicated several congregations. These ex-communicated churches installed women as pastors. Can you believe that? So, because it refused to accept women in all levels of ministry, the white church must preach about the deliverance of the captives.

The black church also must preach deliverance to the captives. Our church has no room to point our fingers at the White Church. Now, there are Black churches that still do not allow women to preach in their church pulpits. Do you think women in these churches need to protest and resist this practice of not supporting women at all levels of ministry?

Dr. Reuben Green, my Pastor, served as Senior Pastor of the Central Baptist Church in Memphis, Tennessee. He was there for nearly forty years. I was ordained there to teach, preach, and serve all of God's people.

On several occasions, Pastor Green stated, "If the women decide to leave this church, I am going right with them". Women are most of the members of any church. And you know, if the women of this church decided that they would leave this church, I am going with them. Our church must preach deliverance. In the church, "There is neither Jew nor Gentile, neither slave nor free, nor is there male and female, for you are all one in Christ Jesus" (Gallatin 3:28).

The preacher must preach about the deliverance of the captives. However, some churches do not want the preacher to preach about the deliverance of the captives. This church may turn me off or put me out for preaching about deliverance, but the church did not call me to preach. God is the one who called me to preach. So, anytime I see and experience sin and evil in God's world, I will preach against it. I must preach for deliverance. I want to go from ghetto to greatness.

Now, our text suggests that we **can go from the ghetto**

to greatness by preaching the acceptable year of the Lord. Jesus preached about the acceptable year of the Lord. Jesus preached that the acceptable year of the lord included the love of self, love for others, and love for God. So, Jesus knew every day was acceptable of the Lord.

The acceptable year of the Lord is any year we are willing to do right. The acceptable year of the Lord is when everyone knows that good comes to those who love God and know that they are called according to the purpose of God. The acceptable year of the Lord is when everyone knows He was wounded for our transgressions and bruised for our iniquities: the chastisement of our peace was upon him, and with his stripes, we are healed. The acceptable year of the Lords is when "Hast thou not know? Has not heard that the everlasting God, the Lord, the Creator of the ends of the earth fainteth not, neither is weary? He giveth power to the faint; and to them that have not might he increaseth strength. Even the youth shall faint and be weary, and the young men shall utterly fall, but they that wait upon the Lord shall renew their strength; they shall mount up with wings as eagles; they shall run, and not be weary; and they shall walk, and not faint. I hear Jesus preaching that The acceptable year of the Lord is when Every valley shall be exalted, and every mountain and hill shall be made low; the crooked shall be made straight, and the rough places plain; and the glory of the Lord shall be revealed, and all flesh shall see it together: for the mouth of the Lord has spoken it.

Oh Yes! Jesus went from the ghetto to greatness. Jesus had faith in tough times. Jesus preached about the deliverance of the captives. And Jesus preached about the acceptable year of the Lord. Oh Yes. Jesus is the classic case of going from the ghetto to greatness. And, I must tell you the reason for this, namely. Jesus is love.

Father
Help your children
And don't let them fall
By the side of the road, mmm
And teach them
To love one another
That Heaven might find
A place in their hearts
'Cause Jesus is love
He won't let you down
And I know He's mine forever
Oh, in my heart
We've got to walk on
Walk on through temptation
'Cause His love and His wisdom
Will be our helpin' hand
And I know the Truth
And His words will be our salvation
Lift up our hearts
To be thankful and glad
That Jesus is love
He won't let you down
And I know He's mine
Deep down in my soul
Jesus is love
Oh, yes, He is
He won't let you down

And I know He's mine, He's mine, He's mine, He's mine, all mine

Forever, oh, in my heart
Help me, heart, heart
Ooh, ooh
I know, I know, I know, I know
Ah, 'cause His love's the power (power)
His love's the glory (glory)
Forever (ever and ever)
Ooh, yeah (yeah, yeah)
Ooh, yeah (yeah, yeah)
Ooh, yeah, yeah (yeah, yeah)
I wanna follow your star
Wherever it leads me
And I don't mind, Lord
I hope you don't mind
I wanna walk with you
And talk with you
And do all the things you want me to do
'Cause I know that Jesus
I know, Lord
(And if you ask, I'll) show
(Love is the word) forever and ever and ever
Who can bring you love? (Jesus)
Who can bring you joy (Jesus)
Who can turn your life around (Jesus), oh
Ooh, yeah (Yeah, yeah)
Yeah (Yeah, yeah, yeah, yeah)
Hey
Who will pick you up? (Jesus)

Ooh, when you fall (Jesus)
Who'll stand beside you? (Jesus)
Who will love us all?
Hey, hey, Jesus (yeah, yeah)
Jesus (yeah, yeah)
Oh, yeah (yeah, yeah)
One thing I wanna say
Who can heal your body? (Jesus)
Who can make it strong? (Jesus)
Who can help you to hold out? (Jesus)
A little while longer
Ooh, yeah (yeah, yeah)
Yeah (yeah, yeah)
Jesus loves you (Yeah, yeah)
Jesus wants you
If you call Him, He will answer
(Jesus) Call him in the mornin'
(Jesus) Call him in the evenin'
(Jesus) Call him in the midnight hour
Hey, hey (yeah, yeah)
Yeah (yeah, yeah)
Yeah, yeah (yeah, yeah)
Yeah, y'all say it
(Jesus is love)

JUDGES CHAPTER 4:1-9

A Multitalented Woman: A Tribute to The Two Porch Founders

I want to preach this morning on the subject, "A Multitalented Woman." This sermon recognizes the contributions of all women. But I want to preach this sermon as a tribute to Kate McDougall and Suzanne Felts. They are Co-Founders of the Porch. Of course, the Porch is composed of a community of various writers. I am a member of the Porch because I am trying endlessly to become a better writer and a more effective preacher.

I read from the Old Testament in Judges, Chapter 4, verses 1 through 9. I am reading from the New King James translation of scripture. "When Ehud was dead, the children of Israel again did evil in the sight of the Lord. So, the Lord sold them to Jabin, King of Canaan, who reigned in Hazor. The Commander of his army was Sisera, who dwelt in Harosheth Hagoyim. And the children of Israel cried out to the Lord; for Jabin had nine hundred chariots of iron, and for twenty years had harshly oppressed the children of Israel. Now, Deborah, a prophetess, the wife of

Lapidoth, was judging Israel at that time. And she would sit under the palm tree of Deborah between Ramah and Bethel in the mountain of Ephraim. And the children of Israel came up to her for judgment. Then she sent and called for Barak, the son of Abinoam from Kadesh in Naphtali, and aid in him, "Has not the Lord God of Israel commanded, "Go and deploy troops at Mount Tabor; take with you ten thousand men of sons of Naphtali and the sons of Zebulun; and against you I will deploy Sisera, the commander of Jabin's army, with his chariots and his multitude at the River Kishon; and I will deliver him into your hand?" And Barak said to her, "If you go with me, then I will go; but if you do not go with me, I will not go". Deborah said I will surely go with you; nevertheless, there will be no glory for you in the journey you are taking, for the Lord will sell Sisera into the hands of a Woman. Then Deborah arose and went with Barak to Kadesh".

James Brown was called affectionately Soul Brother Number One. He was a fascinating singer, performer, and mind-bottling entertainer. James Brown had a song called "It Is a Man's World." But he said, "This world would be nothing without a woman."

Here is our text. Deborah lived and existed within a man's world, but she did not take a second seat to any woman or man. Deborah covered the ground she walked upon. She could do so many different things and yet maintain her balance. Almost nothing bothered her or got under her skin. Deborah was a multitalented woman.

Deborah was a fascinating leader in a trying, challenging, and difficult time in Israel's history. This was the period of the Judges. Other judges included Gideon, Abimelech, and

Samson. But Deborah was the only female judge that we have a record of.

Most importantly, she was a wife, a mother, and a military advisor. A man named Lippoth was Deborah's faithful and devoted husband. And there is nothing to suggest that Deborah did not have any children. She undoubtedly had several children. Nevertheless, as a female judge, Deborah had all her business together. Indeed, I must admit no challenge and no problem was too tricky for Deborah.

Sister Deborah is revealed as a multi-talented woman who demonstrated that she was a fantastic team player. Sister Deborah could walk and chew gum at the same time. She was a superb and superior team player. Magic Johnson was a 6 feet 9 inches basketball player. He played college Basketball for Michigan State University. Magic led Michigan State University to the National College Athletic Association Basketball (NCAA) Championship. He led his team against Larry Bird and the Indiana State University Men's Basketball Team. Magic and his team defeated Larry Bird and the Indiana State University Men's Basketball Team.

Then, Magic became the Los Angeles Lakers' one draft pick, and as a rookie, Magic Johnson helped the Los Angeles Lakers win the National Basketball Association Championship. But do you know why Magic Johnson's teams won those basketball championships? Magic Johnson was a team player.

Deborah was a team player who had the ball of victory in her hand. So, She advises Barak, her military leader, on what to do. Deborah says, "Barak, God told me to tell you what to do. "God commands you: Go take with you ten thousand men and go down to Mount Tabor. And I will lure the enemy Sisera to the Kishon River and give them into your hands."

I hear Brother Barak saying, "No, Sister Deborah, if you go with me, I will go; if you don't go with me, I will not go. So, She says, Brother (General) Barak, Okay! I will go with you". Deborah was a team player.

Listen! We can discern and learn something from Deborah's magnificent and marvelous example. If we want our church, if we want our home, or if we want our relationship to become victorious, we need to become team players. We all must do our part to do what needs to be done.

Deborah helped her people to achieve victory. She was not concerned about the spotlight being on her. Instead, Sister Deborah was concerned that the spotlight fell on her people. Sister Deborah was a team player.

God called Deborah to perform a unique and significant task. She called to help her people reestablish and reconnect their broken covenant relationship with Almighty God. Well. What was this covenantal relationship? Here is that covenant relationship

> Hear O Israel: The Lord our God; the Lord is one. Love the Lord your God with all your heart and with your soul, and with all your strength. These commandments that I give you today are upon your hearts. Impress them on your children. Talk about them when you sit at home, walk

along the road, lie down, and get up. Tie
them as symbols on your hands and bind
them on your foreheads. Write them on
the doorframes of your houses and gates
(Deuteronomy 6:4-9).

The children of Israel did something that they should
not have done. They broke their covenant relationships
with God. And so, They did evil in the eyes of God. They
began to worship other Gods. They began to worship
their things. They began to worship their clothes. They
began worshipping their diamond rings, watches, and other
diamonds. They began to worship their homes. They began
to worship their jobs.

When the children of Israel broke their covenant
relationship, here is what God did. God called Deborah
to bring her people back to their senses. Deborah was the
quintessential team player.

Now, whenever God's people turn their back on God,
God always has someone to speak words on God's behalf.
Oh Yes! Those of us who are members of a church or
congregation have made a covenant with God. Listen, my
sisters and brothers, "We engage, therefore, by the aid of
the Holy Spirit, to walk together in Christian love; to strive
for the advancement of this church in knowledge, holiness,
and comfort."

But some of us here have forsaken and broken our
covenant relationship with God. We are not doing what
God has asked and required of us.

Now, God always has someone to speak to us on God's

behalf. Are you listening to God's preacher? God is calling all of us to reestablish and reconnect to God.

Sister Deborah was also a multi-talented woman who was a dynamic problem solver. Dr. Harry Emerson Fosdick asked, "Are We Part of the problem or part of the answer"? He was asking "Are we the problem solver?

A problem solver has several characteristics. These characteristics include being undaunting, optimistic, driven, intelligent, and empathetic. Deborah possessed these characteristics. She was not part of the problem. Instead, Deborah was a problem solver.

But, in contrast to the problem solver, we know people who are part of the problem. In the Old Testament, Jezebel was part of the problem. She fought against God's prophets. Elijah hid in a cave because Jezebel worked feverishly and intently to destroy all of God's prophets. Sister Jezebel was part of the problem. Donald Trump, the former twice-impeached president, is an example of a being part of the problem. He led a bloodthirsty mob in Washington, D. C, to attack and destroy all vestiges of American Democracy. Vladimir Putin is part of the problem. He is a rootless dictator in Russia. He ordered the Russian military to attack and destroy the innocent people of Ukraine. He is bloodthirsty for more power throughout the world. Putin is part of the problem. The devil is part of the problem. The devil tempted Jesus while he was out in the wilderness. I hear the devil saying, "Jesus if you would fall and worship me, I give you Nashville, Tennessee, and all the world". And I want you to know and understand something. Please do not fool yourself. The devil, evil, and sin are real problems.

Edgar Sheffield Brightman taught theology and

philosophy at Boston University. He authored a book entitled *The Problem of God*. Brightman insisted that God is good. God is powerful and all-knowing, but because of God's goodness and love for us, God decides to limit God's power to allow us to work with God as coworkers to solve problems.

Oh Yes! Deborah worked as a coworker with God to become a problem solver. She had an office designed and positioned where she helped her people to solve problems. She had a comfortable and fashionable office located under a palm tree. But, you know, it did not matter where Deborah's office was. Her office could have been in a dump, a hog pin, a mountaintop, or a valley. The people knew that Deborah could help them solve their problems.

Deborah helped to solve all kinds of problems: Marriage Problems, Siblings problems, Teenage problems, Children's problems, Senior Citizen problems, Dating Problems, etc.

Well. Deborah can help us solve or resolve your dating problem or any other problem. Deborah was not a part of the problem. Instead, she was a problem solver who also operated an effective referral service. Deborah always referred her people to the ultimate problem solver. God is the ultimate problem solver. Oh Yes! God is able. Oh Yes. God is able.

God is able; God is able.
God is able, and God won't fail
Tell me, who can make a mountain
Move out of my way.
And who can make a miracle?
Because of my faith

And when the doctor says no
Who can still say yes
And when I'm in trouble
Who's right there to help me pass every test
God is able, God is able
God is able, and God won't fail
Tell me, who can make a river
Out of a little stream
And who can tell the clouds?
To roll back so that the sun can look at me
And who can tell the wind to whistle through the trees?
And when I'm in trouble, who is the same God
That will come down and rescue me
God is able; God is able
God is able, and He won't fail
He won't fail
He won't fail.
Don't you dare give up
Don't you dare give in
God won't fail.
God is able, God is able.
Tell you God is able, and He won't
God won't, He won't fail.
God won't, He'll never leave.
Never forsake you
No, He won't fail.
He'll be there till the end.
God won't fail; he won't fail.

Deborah had a connection with God because she was a multi-talented woman. Deborah was a problem solver.

Deborah was a team player. Oh Yes! Deborah knew that there was no failure in God. Do you know that there is no failure in God?

In God there is no failure
(God) will do (God will do)
Whatever you ask God to
Just have faith (just have faith)
And believe (and believe)
Many blessings you will receive
For there is no failure, no failure (in God)
Oh, there's never been a time
In my life (God) let me fall.
There's never been a time
(God) did not answer my call
There is no failure
There is no failure in God
Vamp:
(God) will never fail you,
You can believe what (God) said 'cause it's true
(God) will never fail you,
You can believe what (God) said 'cause it's true
Hear you when you call
Catch you when you fall
Just have faith, (God) we'll be right there
There is no failure
There is no failure in God

Printed in the United States
by Baker & Taylor Publisher Services